MAYBE AN Artist

A Graphic Memoir by

LIZ MONTAGUE

RANDOM HOUSE **STUDIO**
NEW YORK

All rights reserved. Published in the United States by Random House Studio,
an imprint of Random House Children's Books,
a division of Penguin Random House LLC, New York.

Random House Studio with colophon is a registered trademark of
Penguin Random House LLC.
Visit us on the Web! GetUnderlined.com
Educators and librarians, for a variety of teaching tools,
visit us at RHTeachersLibrarians.com

Library of Congress Cataloging-in-Publication Data is available upon request.
ISBN 978-0-593-30781-6 (hardcover) — ISBN 978-0-593-30782-3 (pbk.) —
ISBN 978-0-593-30784-7 (ebook)

The text of this book is set in 13-point Liz's Font.
The illustrations were rendered digitally.
Book design by Carol Ly and Juliet Goodman

MANUFACTURED IN CHINA
10 9 8 7 6 5 4 3 2 1
First Edition

TO MY FAMILY, MY HUSBAND,
AND MY NINE-YEAR-OLD SELF.
THANK YOU (FOR EVERYTHING).

I'm a person who was born in a certain place,
in a certain time, and I can be unsure about everything,
but I am not unsure of what I have lived. I know it.

—MARJANE SATRAPI

INTRODUCTION

Do you know how hard it is for your job to be creating something from nothing?!

There's no equation to solve or problem to fix. It's just, like, here's a blank page. Fill it.

Why do I do this?!

GOLDFINCH ELEMENTARY SCHOOL

MARLTON, NEW JERSEY
2001–2007

On September 11, 2001, I was five years old and lived in Marlton, New Jersey, with my parents and two older sisters. That day there was a plane crash two hours away in New York City.

At first, I really didn't think it was a big deal. September 12 felt like any other day.

But things changed the way a day goes to sleep as fall and wakes up as winter. When one leaf on the ground becomes a million leaves.

I got the majority of my news updates from the older kids after school while I waited for the bus home.

I tried to fact-check with my parents, but they didn't understand.

And my teachers didn't understand that my parents didn't understand.

By third grade, the war was old news.

She had a point. Time was marching on in our little world.

When I got home from school, I kept thinking about career day.

Other people had a hard time reading my writing. My parents used a mirror to read it.

My sisters thought my writing was really weird.

Olivia was two years older than me and already in middle school, and Rachel, who was six years older than me, was in high school.

I didn't really notice the direction letters faced. They looked the same both ways to me.

But I didn't just read differently. I spoke differently too.

I became determined to write and speak like everyone else.
I didn't want to fight with my mouth in front of the whole class.

Letters were hard, but shapes were easy. I was really good
at shapes.

By the end of fifth grade, I'd gotten the hang of it.

Mostly.

These are different pictures. They don't match— I can't make these match!

Seeing letters as little pictures meant I had trouble finding connections between capital and lowercase letters.

31

Once elementary graduation came, I hoped I was leaving tests behind once and for all. Middle school would have a more sophisticated system—I was sure of it.

Only, I wasn't excited, I was nervous. Elementary school felt nice and worn in, like a cozy sweater.

Hurston Middle would be stiff and new. I wasn't sure I would fit.

But first came summer. Summer was the best. Summer meant track practice and Girl Scouts and that tight feeling your skin gets after a really hot day.

Summer also meant camp. Rachel, Olivia, and I all went to the same local camp, called the Blue Barn.

We wore bright yellow shirts and mostly ran around outside. Sometimes the older kids hung out with us, like our family friend Joe.

I learned a lot at camp.

That night, I held a family meeting.

I had to do something, anything. I grabbed my markers and got to work. I loved making signs, especially now that other people could easily read my words.

That weekend, with Olivia as my assistant, I hit the streets.

37

I couldn't understand how grown-ups had let things get <u>so</u> bad. Naturally, I wanted answers.

I had never thought much about journalism before. I didn't read the newspapers my dad had lying around—the spacing between letters and words was too small. Sometimes I read global warming articles on my mom's laptop.

I wanted to understand the bigger things going on in the world. Being a journalist seemed like a good way of doing that.

This is the room of

♥ Liz Montague ♥
⭐ Journalist ⭐

But I wasn't going to write tiny-spaced articles. I would make signs. That way everyone could read them.

I spent the rest of the summer mastering my craft.

You never know when you're going to come across a story, so I had to be prepared at all times.

I took journalism so seriously, I even investigated Rachel's room to look for potential stories.

The biggest book on her shelf immediately caught my eye.

I didn't read the whole book, and I didn't finish most of the paragraphs I read, but I understood the gist of it enough to be outraged.

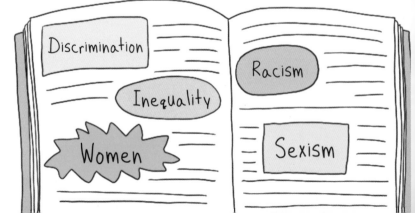

Sadly, my investigation was cut short.

But I had seen plenty.

It was my duty as a journalist to share my newfound information with the public. I ran to my crayon box and worked tirelessly. It felt like years passed.

With this piece, I wanted to communicate injustice, toxic beauty standards, the ethics of capitalism, and so much more.

this is the room of

♡ Liz Montague ♡♡

✗ ~~Journalist~~ ✗

★ Artist ★

HURSTON MIDDLE SCHOOL

MARLTON, NEW JERSEY
2007–2010

A lot changed over the summer. All the brunettes in my class were now blond and had things called highlights.

I had grown two inches and was now offensively tall. And there was a new pause between when I thought something and when I said it.

Every action I took now felt observed, so I began to observe myself. I wasn't walking to math—I was watching myself walk to math. Nothing but bony legs and long strides that became even longer and quicker when I realized everyone else was also watching me walk to math.

Just get to math.
Just get to math.
Just get to math.

I was on display against my will. I stood out from all the other girls in my classes.

I wish my hair were straight. . . .

After school, I borrowed Olivia's hair straightener. I wanted my hair to be flippy and bouncy like the other girls'.

The next morning, my hair looked awful. I was sure my day couldn't get any worse.

Then, to my horror, I was handed a Scantron test.

Sixth grade was not off to a great start.

Dear Diary,
   Middle School
is pretty awful.
   They have tests!!

My grades are
not great, but my
parents still got
me a dog, which
I didn't expect.

We're still getting used to each other. I named her Timmy after Timmy Turner from "Fairly Odd Parents." I think she likes her name.

JINGLE JINGLE

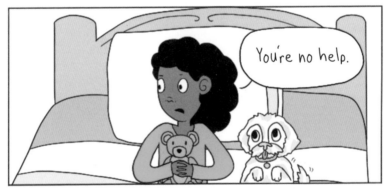

The next day at lunch, I decided sixth grade was officially the worst.

Usually I sat at a back table with girls I knew from Girl Scouts, but that day their table was full.

Hey, can I sit and eat here?

Sure!

I sat in the same spot every day for a few weeks, and it officially became My Table. I, Elizabeth Montague, had a table. I even started making friends with the girls who sat there.

Have you heard of this new Facebook thing?

What's Facebook?

It's this website that's like a people dictionary—

but with people we actually know.

My older sisters had Myspace, but I'd never had any interest in that. As soon as I got home, though, I checked out Facebook. It was an entirely new frontier.

It was nice being able to meet people without actually having to meet them and know things about them without actually having to talk to them.

A lot of things changed in 2008.

Sixth grade felt small.

The school year rolled to a stop like a marble on flat ground.

What is "HAGS"?

"Have a Great Summer"!

Summer started with Rachel leaving.

She got an athletic scholarship for school, and practice was beginning right away.

Can I have your room since you're leaving?

No! I still live here—I'm just going to college.

Can I have Rachel's room?

Yeah, sure.

I can't believe Rachel's really gone!

SHE JUST LEFT!

Summer always starts fun and gets boring really quickly. I decided to ask Olivia to get me a job.

You steal Rachel's room on the day she moves out, and now I'm supposed to do **you** a favor?

Yeah.

She worked at a farm up the road a few hours a week. She got free doughnuts and could afford to go to the movies with her friends.

A few weeks later, I started my new job.

First day of work! I'm so excited! This is so grown-up!

I have a reputation to uphold— don't embarrass me.

Me? Embarrass you?!

I advocated for myself during my next shift later that week.

Play area is **great**, but is there anything else I can try?

I know just the thing!

HA HA HA

Toward the end of summer, my luck started to change.

Sarah called out sick.
Do you want
to be on birthday
parties today?

YES!

Birthday parties were the big leagues. Our job was mostly to
just help set up and watch the kids, but afterward we usually
got cake or pizza if there were any leftovers.

Do you need help
with anything?

Do you have signs
so guests know
where to come?

LIZ

Summer flew by after that, and seventh grade started with a bang.

Having a cell phone officially cemented my place in middle school society. I was on the edge of thirteen with a job to go to (only on the weekends) and friends to text. A boy to text too.

A boy named Patrick. He went by Pat, just like how I went by Liz instead of Elizabeth. We had so much in common.

Patrezio38: hey

Trackgurlxoxo: hey

Patrezio38: wats up

Trackgurlxoxo: nmu?

Patrezio38: nm

Trackgurlxoxo: cool

Patrezio38: cool

We were in the same grade, so I saw him around a lot, but I was much better onscreen than I was in person.

We definitely liked each other, but it was complicated.

You guys look nice together — translated to — The only two Black kids in school must be soul mates.

The annoying part was maybe we **were** soul mates.

OMG I'm doing homework too!

but I didn't want everyone thinking we were soul mates just because we were both Black.

My town was not a hub of diversity.

With the exception of the first two weeks of any US history class, I usually felt invisible. My classmates did the same choreography every time:

But others had it worse than me, and not just during the slavery talk, but all the time. I guess if I had to choose, I'd rather be invisible than be called a terrorist.

But I was angry that I had to choose. I felt like my white classmates (especially the boys) were allowed to be ignorant, but I wasn't.

LIZ
Does it ever bother you?

PAT
What?

LIZ
That white kids can do and say whatever they want and we can't.

PAT
You could if you wanted. I do.

LIZ
It's not the same, and you know it!

PAT
You're overthinking this.

I had no desire to bully people or be mean, but being so aware was exhausting.

I talked to my sister about it when I got home from school.

Why are boys allowed to be so mean?

Allowed?

These boys were saying awful things to another boy in class, and all I could think was where is their little voice and why are they allowed to ignore it?

If you hear voices, you've got bigger problems than boys in class.

No, not like that! The little voice that's supposed to read everyone's mind around you. Like "Don't say this or so-and-so will feel this way" or "Don't do that or this could happen." I thought everybody had it.

Maybe they were joking and the other boy was in on it.

They weren't, and he wasn't. I could tell.

Kids are going to be mean sometimes. That's just life.

Yes, but why are certain kids allowed to not know how their actions impact others?

And the rest of us get stuck with little voices that try to read minds?

I didn't mean to draw anything while we talked. I was just doodling on what was supposed to be homework.

I liked the
doodle enough to
put it in the cover
of my school binder
the next day.

What if people ask
what the picture
means?

I hope
they do!

And the more I thought about it, the more I realized doodling really helped me think.

I know we're supposed to do a book report, but is it okay if I draw a book presentation instead?

As long as you follow the rubric, I'm open to it.

After that, I drew every assignment I could.

My classes were becoming much more manageable, but extracurriculars were becoming more and more important to my future. I'd done sports my entire life.

BASKETBALL

FIELD HOCKEY

GYMNASTICS

SOFTBALL

But track was different.

(Summer before eighth grade)

When I started track

When I started making track friends

When I realized I was good at track

When I realized I was expected to get an athletic scholarship like my sister Rachel did

I was always tired.

I didn't mind track, it was just—

Four years in high school, then four years in college—that's eight years! Eight years of running?!

So much potential!

Just like her sister!

Drive.

She has to want it.

Full scholarship!

Effort.

For eighth grade superlatives, I was voted Most Athletic.

Which was cool, I guess.

Sometimes it feels like people already have their minds made up about me before they even know me. Even when they do know me!

Like there's a lens between the real me and whoever it is they think I am.

I thought a lot about how people saw me versus how I saw myself.

How do I get everyone else inside my head?

DIARY

Or should I make my own little world and keep everyone else out?

High school me will
have more answers....

I hope.

GREEN RIVER
HIGH SCHOOL

MARLTON, NEW JERSEY
2010–2014

My first few weeks of ninth grade, something strange began to happen.

I knew my quest,

but I didn't know I'd become
invisible along the way.

And I don't think anybody noticed that I was becoming invisible.

Green River High had over 4,000 students, five times as many as Hurston Middle.

LIZ

I didn't think things would be this different.

LIZ

Even girls I went to Goldfinch Elementary with seem like total strangers.

LIZ

Hello?

LIZ

Pat?

LIZ

. . .

I don't really care.
Everyone just put me
and Pat together because
we're both Black.
We're not soul mates.
We're barely even friends.
We're nothing.
It doesn't matter.
No one ever ends up
with someone from middle
school, so it would've
been a waste of my time.

A total w
I don't car
We're n
He can
Whatever h
Doesn't ma
It's tota

DIARY

It turns out invisible people move faster through time.

How are we supposed to read 400 pages in two days and go to six-hour practices. Like for what?!

It's so unnecessary and we just do it like it makes sense, but none of it makes sense!

Why don't we learn something useful, like how to do taxes or pay a mortgage?!

No—that would make too much sense. Learning about dead Russian authors is totally useful.

Maybe if we learned practical things, society wouldn't be such a mess.

Realizing I just had a meltdown in front of the whole class.

I'm sorry, I didn't mean to interrupt class. I promise it won't happen again.

I need to get an athletic scholarship, and art schools don't have good enough sports programs to give decent money.

And I don't know . . .

I didn't even really like this "blur-motion" idea. I just picked it because I had to pick something, and then I wasted a year making work I don't even like.

That doesn't mean art school would be a waste. This year was just a skill year.

I don't think art school is a waste at all. I just don't know if I'm good at making art on demand.

But what I didn't say was that I wasn't just unsure about art school—I was unsure about college as a whole.

I felt like I wasn't good at doing anything on demand.
I couldn't understand how everyone already knew what they
wanted to do with their life.

I mean, it's not that outrageous. Plenty of people don't go to college.

How much of this is stuff we **actually** want versus what we're expected to do?

I don't even know what I want to do.

I don't really think I'm a "school" person.

I just— I mean— you know—

There are a lot of paths out there beyond this one way of doing things.

The older I got, the less I had a summer.

Instead I had practice and college visits and SAT prep.

LIZ
The house feels too quiet

OLIVIA
You can always come visit me and Rachel

LIZ
I will

OLIVIA
:)

By the end of junior year, I'd broken nearly all of Rachel's school records. I was getting heavily recruited, and with each recruiting letter I became more panicked.

I didn't have a dream school or a major I was super passionate about. I just didn't want to let anyone down.

Picking a school felt like the most important decision of my life, the foundation I would build my adulthood on.

Pat texted me today out of the blue.
He's staying in NJ for college.
I want to get as far away from here as possible. I can't believe he wants to stay.

I guess I don't really know him anymore, though. Not really.
We've been on different planets since middle school.

I wonder how Middle School Liz would feel about all this (sometimes I think my younger self knew more).

Remember when drawing was fun?
Maybe it still could be. . . .

131

I still have time, right?

Right?!

3 ½ YEARS LATER

RICHMOND, VIRGINIA

I started posting little drawings of me and Timmy on Instagram over the last few days.

(Just to help me sort out my own thoughts, really.)

Just do your best!

I've been calling it "Liz at Large" for now, but I might change the name.

Someone came up to me in the dining hall at dinner and told me they loved the drawings. It legit made my day. ♡

143

144

MAJOR DECLARATION

Name : Elizabeth (Liz) Montague

Major : Studio Art

I keep waiting for one big thing to change it all.

You're one big thing.

~~AFTERWORD~~

ADULTING

But they are made up of people. I wonder if there's a person in there who'd even listen.

Probably not—who even cares? It's not your job to care about this.

But it could be your job to care . . . if you wanted it.

I guess I could send an email, but it doesn't even matter. Nothing is going to come from this.

To: New Yorker Cartoon Dept.

Subject: Something to be aware

Hi.

I don't know if you're aware, but your cartoons . . .

I need to get back to work.

To: New Yorker Cartoon Dept.

Subject: Re: Something to be aware of

Hi, Emma.

I'd like to recommend myself. I've been drawing my entire life, and you can see my portfolio at . . .

— She has no idea!

What are you talking about?

MY NEW YORKER CARTOONS (!!)

PER MY LAST E-MAIL

LIZ MONTAGUE

"We've done all we can. It's out of our hands now."

That was my first New Yorker cartoon!!

One of my favorites!

I love the bunny ☺

How to Teach Your Parents Sustainability

LIZ MONTAGUE

"And then the princess gave up her throne, because she didn't believe in social stratification."

"I think the universe is trying to tell me something."

Obama Foundation

OBAMA.ORG

Michelle Obama posted this on her Instagram.
MICHELLE LAVAUGHN ROBINSON OBAMA!!!

Artwork by Liz Montague

us open

IBM

Home : News : Black Lives To The Front: Liz Montague

Presented by

Black Lives To The Front: Liz Montague

U.S. Open

ACKNOWLEDGMENTS

Thank you to this project for being there during 2020 when I really needed something to hold on to.

Thank you to Annie Kelley, my amazing editor, for your humor and unwavering confidence in me. I'm so grateful I got to do my first book with you! Thank you to Wendi Gu, my incredible agent, for always being a guiding light full of understanding and care. Thank you to Carol Ly for your hard work on this project that did not go unnoticed! You all were absolutely vital in this book coming to fruition.

Mom and Dad, thank you for keeping me in art and sports and out of trouble and putting me in a position to make good choices (even when I fought tooth and nail against it). Olivia and Rachel, thanks for always keeping it real and doing the hard stuff first so I knew it was possible. I'm eternally grateful that we all get to do this journey together, and I love you guys.

Pat, thank you for pep talks, the constant shoulder to cry on, and being the best person to laugh with. Thank you for building a life with me that makes my dreams possible.

Thank you to my amazing friends Steph, Sarah, Shelby, Nene, Whitney, and so many others for all the Facetimes, texts, and phone calls. I'm so grateful for your love and support.

Thank you to Tanja Softic, Jeremy Drummond, Dr. David Stevens, and Dr. Monti Datta for teaching me the power of craft and purpose.

Thank you to Mrs. Wilson (may she rest in peace), Mrs. Henning, Mr. Ellis, Mrs. Delguercio, and every art teacher, educator, and coach I've been lucky to have.

To anyone who reads this book, thank you for reading it. I hope it finds you at the exact place and time it's meant to.

With gratitude and love,

Liz

Liz Montague is a cartoonist, writer, and illustrator whose work focuses on the intersection of self and social awareness. She began contributing cartoons to the *New Yorker* in 2019, at the age of twenty-two. She has also illustrated for the Biden presidential campaign, the Obama Foundation, Google, the Food Network, the US Open, and more. Liz is the creator of the popular *Liz at Large* cartoon series, which ran in *Washington City Paper*, and is passionate about documenting social change and social movements. She fundamentally believes in representation, accessible information, and drawing your feelings. This is her first children's book. Liz lives in Philadelphia with her husband, Pat (yes, *that* Pat!).

lizatlarge.org   @lizatlarge   lizatlarge